My problem with Christianity is . . .

MY PROBLEM WITH CHRISTIANITY IS...

Paul Weston

Harold Shaw Publishers
Wheaton, Illinois

© Paul Weston, 1991, original edition under the title *Why
We Can't Believe*. Harold Shaw edition, © Paul Weston, 1992,
is published by special arrangement with Inter-Varsity
Press, 38 DeMontfort Street, Leicester LE1 7GP England.

Cover design and art © 1992 by Turnbaugh & Associates

ISBN 0-87788-576-1

Library of Congress Cataloging-in-Publication Data

Weston, Paul, 1957-
    My problem with Christianity is— / Paul Weston.
        p.   cm.
    British ed. published under title: Why we can't believe.
©1991.
    Includes bibliographical references.
    ISBN 0-87788-576-1
    1. Apologetics—20th century. I. Title. II. Title: Why we
can't believe.
BT1102.W473 1992   91-37432
                                      CIP

99 98 97 96 95 94 93 92

10 9 8 7 6 5 4 3 2 1

Contents

Introduction ___ *vii*

1. "There's no proof!"___*1*

2. "Christianity is irrelevant"___*15*

3. "I've never really thought about it"___*27*

4. "The biggest obstacle is the church"___*41*

5. "There's so much suffering in the world"___*51*

6. "Christianity can't be the only way to God"___*63*

Conclusion ___*75*

If you want to read more ___*77*

Notes ___*79*

Introduction

This is a book about "obstacles."

We asked over six hundred people between the ages of eighteen and thirty the question: *"What is the biggest obstacle that prevents you from believing in Christianity?"*

We didn't give them a number of possible answers to choose from since we didn't want to influence what they said in any way. We simply wanted to find out what people *really* think—not what *we* think they might be thinking!

The people who talked to us came from a wide cross section of class, color, and creed within society. Some were students, others were professional people. Some had paid jobs or worked in the home. Others were unemployed. But all had something to say.

Some of the people we met were already Christians. But we also met many who were not. It is for them that this book has been written.

We recorded what they said to us and then tried to sort the replies into categories. As it turned out, this was easier than we anticipated. The replies fell into a number of main groups, and for each group a "representative reply" was identified that seemed to sum up the responses in that group. These "representative" replies form the chapter

headings of this book. They represent the six most popular
replies that we received.

In each chapter I've tried to consider the questions that
are actually raised by people's replies. Above all, I've tried
to stick to the point. As a result, the book is not intended
as an overall introduction to Christianity, where the writer
makes one chapter follow logically from the previous one.
You *will* find connections between the different chapters.
(And this is natural because Christianity *does* fit together.)
But that's not the main objective here.

Instead, this is a book that attempts to give some
answers to the biggest obstacles that prevent people from
believing in Christianity today. It's intended to get people
thinking.

If it helps to do that, I will be very pleased.

References to the Bible

For easy reference, quotations from the Bible are set out
with the book title first, followed by the chapter and then
the verse. So for Mark 7:20-22, read the Gospel of Mark,
chapter 7, and verses 20, 21, and 22.

All Bibles have a contents page to help find the various
sections.

chapter

❶

"There's no proof!"

Among the many responses to our survey that we received, this one was the most popular. More than one in every ten of the people asked said that the whole idea of God's existence was a problem for them.

What's the biggest obstacle?

- "I could give you a one-word answer—proof!" —*26-year-old computer programmer*
- "I haven't seen enough proof to justify God's existence." —*24-year-old electrician*

Many want visible evidence:

- "I haven't seen God. I have to see with my own eyes to believe anything."
- "I only believe in what I can see, and I have a very materialistic outlook to life."
- "One's curiosity is rarely satisfied over any subject unless visible evidence can be supplied."

So, as one person put it, "Who's to say? Can you be sure?"

Replies like these could easily be multiplied many times over by people from all walks of life.

Some people are confused by the whole idea of God. John Hurt, the actor, summed it up when he was interviewed in *SHE* magazine a few years ago: "I'm not sure if God created man or if man created God." Others seem to have a very clear idea about what God is like.

So what's the truth? Is it reasonable to suppose that God exists?

Proof

Many people say, "You can't *prove* that God exists." And they are right—you can't. But others might reply, "You can't prove that he doesn't exist either." And they are right too—you can't.

So we must begin by saying that this desire for scientific proof may not get us very far in deciding whether God exists or not.

We all accept the existence of certain things that we cannot scientifically prove: friendship, love. Those who are *in* love with someone will often say it's the most real thing they've ever experienced. Yet they wouldn't be able to prove it scientifically to someone else. There is good evidence, but it stops short of scientific proof. In fact, experts tell us that there are very few things that one can *prove* to be true in a scientific sense. Most of those have to do with complex areas of mathematics and philosophy. And even there we find argument.

The Bible never sets out to prove that God exists. This is partly because his existence is always assumed, but partly because God is not to be understood as some kind of mathematical formula that can be either proved or disproved. He is a personal being. He must be experienced. He must be *met*.

That is why Christians talk about coming to *know* God, about *experiencing* him. They describe him as "Father" and relate to him within a bond of friendship and trust.

"Proof," then, is not a very fruitful idea.

A much more helpful approach is to think in terms of evidence that points to the existence of this personal God. And there's plenty of it—enough, in fact, to come to reliable conclusions.

Clues

Suppose I take you over to my friend Jonathan's house. He's invited us in to take a look at it. He's an architect and has designed every part of the house himself. He's decorated it and chosen all the furniture and fittings to reflect his own taste.

Then suppose there's some delay and he's late arriving. We have half an hour to kill and so have time to look over his house before he comes. I wonder what you'd find out about him. Quite a lot, I'd imagine. You'd discover his taste in color and perspective. You'd find out what kind of music he listens to and what he likes to read. You'd discover all kinds of things.

Even though you haven't met this person you already know something about him.

You might find it helpful to think about the existence of God in a similar sort of way.

If this is God's world you'd expect to find some marks of his ownership within it: clues that lead you to the conclusion that some greater power must be behind it all. We have to ask whether these clues suggest that he *does* exist or whether they're best explained some other way.

Did someone "design" the world or did it fall into place?

Somehow we have to explain the existence of the world itself. How did it get here? Why is it like it is? What explanation best fits the evidence that we see around us?

There are some who argue that it came about as a result of a series of cosmic explosions somewhere in space and at some point in history. By this explanation human life developed by chance. The process was haphazard, like the pattern produced when you take a pile of leaves and toss them in the air.

But does this really satisfy the evidence? We live in a world of infinite variety. John Constable, the landscape artist whose close study of nature is mirrored in many of his famous paintings, said that his careful observation of trees had persuaded him that there could never be "two leaves alike since the creation of the world."

Yet alongside this endless and minute variety there is also an underlying sense of order. The very study of science is possible only because there are certain "fixed" laws that govern how things work. There's the ordered cycle of the seasons, of day and night, light and dark, summer and winter. Are these the product of chance?

Then there's the complexity of creation. Think about the human body. Recent developments in hi-tech digital audio reproduction have focused attention on the capabilities of the human ear. Experts now estimate that it is able to distinguish over one million different sounds. It is far in advance of any human invention. Or take the body's structure. Each one of its sixty million cells performs a series of complex operations and is itself a powerful storehouse of information.

The eminent scientist Sir Fred Hoyle, though himself not a Christian, says in his recent book *The Intelligent Universe* that the chances of any one of our body's 200,000 proteins having evolved by chance are roughly the same as the chances a blindfolded person has of solving Rubik's Cube. Chances that he estimates at 50,000,000,000,000,000,000 to 1![1]

Think of your favorite piece of music. There is a statistical possibility that if you put one hundred monkeys into a locked room with an infinite supply of pencils and manuscript paper one day they could reproduce it. But how much would you bet on it?

Where does the order in our world come from? Does it suggest that we live in a world designed by someone outside it or did it get there by chance? Voltaire, the French thinker, wrote in a letter to a friend, "I shall always be convinced that a watch proves a watchmaker, and that a universe proves a God."

Why do people have a "spiritual" dimension?

The twentieth-century philosopher Bertrand Russell wrote:

> The centre of me is always and eternally a terrible pain—a curious and wild pain—searching for something beyond what the world contains, something transfigured and infinite . . . I do not think it is to be found—but the love of it is my life.[2]

Our lives suggest to us, in one way or another, that we were made for something greater, something more beautiful, more lasting, more real. And people are searching for that "something." It's a curious fact that although God's existence is being questioned today, we live in an age in which people are well aware of the spiritual dimension. The Religious Experiences Research Unit at Nottingham University, England, recently published the results of a survey that shows that well over a third of women and just under a third of men claim to have had "some sort of religious experience."

There is also a hunger for this spiritual reality. This has sometimes been used as an argument against God's existence. Some people say things like, "You only think there's a God because you *want* him to exist—because you have some need for him. It's a sign of weakness."

But the alternative conclusion is surely just as convincing, and, in the end, more likely. Saint Augustine wrote, "You made us for yourself, O God, and our hearts are

restless until they find their rest in you." We reach out for
God because he has put a hunger in us to do so.

No one would dream of saying that food didn't exist
simply because people felt a need for it. Our physical
hunger is there to be satisfied. So is our spiritual hunger.

Where do "values" come from?

Hundreds of books have been written on this subject.
Philosophers, psychiatrists, psychoanalysts, and anthro-
pologists have all put forward their views on the origin of
"values."

The prevailing mood in our day is that you cannot talk
about standards of "right" or "wrong" that come from
"outside" our society. There are no "absolutes." But is this
the experience of ordinary people? Most people have a very
real sense of what is right and wrong, of what is just and
unjust. Take the plight of the starving millions, or the
mugging of a defenseless elderly person, or the sexual
abuse of a child.

And what about our own lives? One of the most common
reactions when a close friend or relative dies is one of
regret: "I wish I hadn't said that," or "I wish I'd done more."

At the end of the day as we look back on all that has
happened—the conversations, the thoughts, reactions, attitudes—which of us can admit we have no regrets about
our performance? Which of us hasn't felt the stab of conscience?

Sue was a bright college junior who came to an informal
discussion group that we were running in a university town
some years ago. She was full of questions. As we went
around the different members of the group, I asked people
to put into words why they had come. When it came to her
turn, Sue said, "I've come to find out the truth. I know that
within myself I have a great potential for good, but I also
know I can do real damage—to myself and to others."

It is, of course, possible to argue that our consciences are
formed and shaped entirely by social patterns within
society. They have nothing to do with a personal God who

is "outside." But what I am suggesting is that it is just as possible—and in fact more likely—that they reflect a higher moral standard, a standard that is reflected in those who are made in the image of a personal God.

Our knowledge of that standard may well have become eroded through misuse, but it is still there.

How do some people claim that God has changed their lives?

It's a fact that most people who become Christians are made to think about it in the first place because of the quality of life they see in others. Jesus said it would be so. He told his followers, "By this all men will know that you are my disciples, if you love one another" (John 13:35). It may be that you have seen this quality in other Christians, too. (Perhaps it is because of this that you are reading this book.)

Life lived in obedient friendship with God is one powerful sign of God's existence. I think of two Iranian students (both called Ali) whom I met a few years ago. They joined a small group to study the claims of Jesus. They became thoroughly absorbed and came along each night to examine the Bible with us. As the days went by there was a seriousness about their questions and an eagerness to find answers. After some time they both came to believe that Christianity was true and both came to believe in Jesus Christ. Then came the time for them to return to Iran. "What will happen to you?" I asked. "Are you sure you know what you are doing?"

It seemed easy for an American to believe in Christianity. There are no threats, no great hassles. But for them? They answered, "We will probably be cut off from our families. We may be put in prison. We may die. But we've found the truth."

So far we've been looking at "clues"—the world's design, the existence of values, a spiritual dimension, and the effect God might be having in the lives of others. I've been suggesting that they point to the existence of a personal God who created the world and has left his marks on it.

But think back to the visit to the architect's house. We know something about him from what he's made. But when he arrives back at the house what we know about him suddenly becomes transformed. We meet the person himself.

The final "clue" is much more than a clue. For, in Jesus Christ, it is claimed that God himself *has* visited us. For a short while, the one who created the world became part of it so that we could meet him personally. If this is true, it surely gives us the greatest evidence that God exists.

What about the life of Jesus?

Some school children were asked to paint a picture about anything they liked. They got messily down to work on their masterpieces and time went by. When they'd finished, the teacher went around the room, looking at each painting in turn. All the pictures were vaguely like human beings who'd been put on severe crash diets. All, that is, except for Tommy's.

"What's that?" she asked, looking at a strange mass of color.

"It's God," he replied.

"But no one knows what God is like," she said.

He looked up with an expression of triumph. "*Now* they do!"

That's exactly what they said about Jesus. "No one has ever seen God," wrote John at the start of his Gospel, but his one and only son "has made him known" (John 1:18).

So how do we handle the evidence?

"Is the evidence reliable?"
Many people ask this: "Weren't the New Testament documents written a long time after Jesus died? And haven't

they been altered over the centuries? How then can we trust them?"

Yes, the documents were written some time after Jesus died—the Gospels probably thirty or more years after, and Paul's letters between twenty and thirty-five years after. But this is still well within the lifetime of most of his contemporaries.

We do not have the original "signed" manuscripts—only copies. But the fact is that there is more early manuscript evidence for the reliability of the New Testament than for any other ancient book that's been written. The histories written by the Greek historian Thucydides are a good example. He lived over four hundred years before Jesus, and his work is only known to us because there are eight copies of the original manuscripts that have survived. The earliest of these is dated at around A.D. 900—over thirteen hundred years after they were first written! Similarly, the earliest copies of the histories written by Tacitus and Julius Caesar are dated around seven hundred and nine hundred years after they were written. Yet no scholar of the period would say that for that reason they are of no historical value. Histories are based on such accounts.

By contrast, the earliest piece of manuscript evidence for the New Testament dates from only about fifty years after it was originally written. And on top of this we possess over five thousand manuscript pieces of various parts of the New Testament. These are so numerous and so comparatively near the original time of writing that they are the envy of experts studying other ancient literature.

So we can approach the New Testament in confidence that it will give us reliable information about Jesus. As Bishop Neill, the New Testament scholar, writes: "Anyone who reads the New Testament . . . in any modern translation, can feel confident that, though there may be uncertainties in detail, in almost everything of importance he is close indeed to the text of the New Testament books as they were originally written."[3]

What do the writers say they're doing?

When we turn to the New Testament records about Jesus we find two remarkable things.

First we find that the authors are concerned to get their facts right. Luke introduces his Gospel to Theophilus (his patron, or sponsor) in this way:

> Many have undertaken to draw up an account of the things that have been fulfilled among us, just as they were handed down to us by those who from the first were eyewitnesses and servants of the world. Therefore, since I myself have *carefully investigated* everything from the beginning, it seemed good also to me to write an *orderly account* for you . . . so that you may know the *certainty* of the things you have been taught. *Luke 1:1-4,* italics mine

Note the desire to get things right.

Second, they mention the evidence of those who were actually there. We all know the importance attached to eyewitnesses, whether in a court of law or on the television news. No sooner has a political crisis arisen, an international disaster occurred, or a war broken out than countless reporters are sent to the scene. Their reports are flashed across our screens. Their evidence carries authority. They were there. They saw it happen.

So when the life of Jesus is recorded, the writers are also concerned to get the facts from people who were *there.* Luke mentions them in the passage above. John says five times in the first nineteen verses of his Gospel that it is based on the evidence of those who saw Jesus for themselves. Papias, an early church historian, records that Mark's Gospel is based on the evidence of the disciple Peter. "Mark . . . wrote down accurately all that he (Peter) remembered." He goes on to record that Mark made it his aim "not to omit anything that he had heard, nor to include any false statement."

What do they say about Jesus?

What kind of man was Jesus Christ? The best way to find out is to read one of the Gospels and see for yourself. Try Mark's Gospel, which is short enough to read through in a couple of hours.

J.B. Phillips, a New Testament translator, describes his reaction to the Gospels as being books that are "alive with power": "I got the deepest feeling that I possibly could have expected," he said. "It changed me . . . I came to the conclusion that these words bear the seal of the Son of Man and God."

Two things about Jesus stand out: the evidence of his claims and the evidence of his resurrection.

The evidence of his claims. Was Jesus God in human form? If he *was*, then the question of God's existence is obviously settled. It would be the strongest possible evidence. It would also be the most helpful because, if God were to show us what he was like by becoming a human being, it would tell us so much more about him than we could tell simply from studying creation.

But was he? The unanimous conclusion of the New Testament writers is that this is the only possible way to describe Jesus. Countless others have also been convinced as they've looked at the evidence. The well-known writer C.S. Lewis wrote to a friend:

> "The doctrine of Christ's divinity seems to me not something stuck on which you can unstick but something that peeps out at every point so that you'd have to unravel the whole web to get rid of it."[4]

In the first place we come across the fact that Jesus kept claiming to be doing things that only God had the power to do. He claimed to be able to forgive people for the wrong things that they were doing to others. He claimed to be the one who would offer salvation to the world through his own death. He claimed that he would rise again from the dead after three days. He claimed to be the one who would judge the entire world one day—and that the destiny of everyone would depend upon their reaction to him.

There was also the way in which he described himself. For one thing he claimed a unique unity with God—something completely scandalous to the Jewish mind (for in their belief there is only one God). But Jesus said, "I and the Father *are* one," "If you've seen me you've *seen* God" (John 10:30; 14:9, paraphrased). C.S. Lewis describes this claim as "the most shocking thing that has ever been uttered by human lips." And to cap it all, he even claimed immortality. He was going to live forever. And he had always existed since the beginning of time (John 8:57-58).

So what does it all add up to? Both his enemies and his friends were unanimous about it. He was claiming to be God.

His enemies put him to death for it. Right from the start this was their charge against him. At one point, as they picked up stones to kill him, they told him they were doing it because of "blasphemy, because you, a mere man, claim to be God" (John 10:33).

The evidence of his resurrection. His friends, on the other hand, came to worship him *as* God. All the things that he said about himself came true. Most remarkable of all was his claim that he would rise again from the dead on the third day after he was put to death. It was the fulfillment of this prediction that fully persuaded them. The apostle Paul wrote to the church in Rome, some twenty years after it happened, that the resurrection is the clearest single indication that Jesus was who he said he was (Romans 1:4). We shall need to examine some of the evidence for this in the next chapter.

Perhaps the most striking piece of evidence for their belief in the divinity of Jesus is the fact that they began to describe him as their "Lord." This Greek word was used to translate the Hebrew name of God in the Old Testament that was so holy that only its consonants were written out ("YHWH"). They, however, used it to apply to Jesus. All of them were Jews. All believed in the essential unity of God. But all had come to recognize that in Jesus Christ, God had become a human being.

■ In summary

Does God exist? And can he be known?

There are many clues that point to the existence of a God whose world we live in. But the New Testament points to the person of Jesus Christ as the clearest evidence that this is the case. It is he who brings God into sharp focus for us. That is why he came.

Russian cosmonauts reported after one space flight, "We've been up to heaven, and there's no one there." But the New Testament declares that you don't have to look into outer space to find God. He has visited us, and you can meet him today in the person of Jesus Christ.

chapter

❷

"Christianity is irrelevant"

- "I don't feel any need to believe."
- "I manage to live without it; I don't need it."
- "It's totally unnecessary to my life."

I heard replies like this many, many times as I talked to people in the survey.

- "I do not find that in my life there is a space for which I need a God." —*27-year-old doctor*
- "Christianity doesn't have any meaning to us young people . . . it doesn't meet our needs." —*28-year-old, unemployed*
- "It's out of date." —*Pre-med student*

Is Christianity a system of outdated beliefs that we can ignore safely? After all, said one person, there are "too many other things in life to worry about."

The answer to the question of whether Christianity is relevant today depends on whether or not Christianity is *true*.

If it *is* true, then Jesus Christ must affect the whole way that we look at the world, at ourselves, and at God. If it *isn't* true, then we needn't really bother about it at all. Some people might like to take it up as a hobby, but it doesn't really matter to them one way or the other. It may keep a few ministers off the street, but for the rest of us it *is* irrelevant.

Truth

People are rightly concerned about truth. One of our basic instincts as human beings is to get at the real truth about the questions and issues that affect our lives. What's the most reliable car? Is my house going to fall down? Am I suffering from an illness that needs urgent treatment? Am I covered by my insurance policy? Am I spending more than I'm earning? Knowing the truth about questions like these will help us to avoid making mistakes. It will mean that we can make reliable decisions. It will help to bring security and certainty into our lives.

So truth is very important.

Christianity claims to give us the truth in a world of uncertainties. In fact, it claims to tell us the answers to the greatest questions that we can ever ask ourselves:

- What will happen when I die?
- Who's in control of the world?
- What's the purpose of life?

If somebody could give you the answers to *these* questions so that you could live on the strength of them, wouldn't you want to know? And if Christianity could be shown to supply the answers, would it not be relevant?

Christians claim that they *have* found the answers to these questions in the person of Jesus Christ. And if you ask how they know, they will point to the startling claim that he rose from the dead three days after he was put to death.

How can this be? Let us examine these questions and ask how the claim that Jesus rose from the dead sheds light on them.

The question of death

When we asked one person in our survey what was the biggest obstacle preventing him from believing in Christianity, he wrote "DEATH" across the reply slip in large capital letters.

The certainty of death awaits every one of us. One in one dies. It's been described as "the ultimate statistic." Benjamin Franklin, the American politician, put it this way: "There is nothing so certain in life as death—and taxes."

But how do we come to terms with this certainty? To many it seems to make a mockery of life's potential. Bishop John Robinson summed it up when he wrote, "If man is on his own in the universe, then beyond a brief span of years for the individual . . . the future is irretrievably bleak." The novelist Peter Shaffer put it like this: "I'm going to die, and the thought of that dark has for years rotted everything for me, all simple joy in life."

As a result many are afraid of death. The Duke of Wellington said that a person "must be a coward or a liar who could boast of never having felt a fear of death." The novelist Tolstoy wrote that to wait for death was something he feared more than anything.

Some try to ignore it and pretend it won't happen. Jack had spent some time in the hospital. He had been on the critical list, but his condition had recently stabilized. As I walked into the ward, the first thing that struck me was the view from the window near his bedside. It looked out over a graveyard. I must have made some remark about it because the thing I remember is how strongly he insisted that it didn't bother him at all. The following week I made a return visit. He'd been moved to another ward. The nurse said, "We didn't want to move him, but he insisted. He said the graveyard was getting on his nerves!"

Is there an answer to the question of death?

The classical Greek writer Aeschylus wrote, "When the earth has drunk up a man's blood, once he is dead, there is no resurrection."

But what if this is not true? What if someone has been through death ahead of us—on our behalf—so that we could live without the ultimate fear of what it might do to us? What if death is no longer the ultimate threat? What then?

Right at the heart of Christianity is the claim that Jesus did just this. Whether it is true or not is clearly of supreme importance.

Did Jesus Christ rise from the dead?

The evidence is very strong indeed. Bishop Westcott, a well-known New Testament scholar of a previous generation, summed it up this way: "It is not too much to say that there is no single historical incident better or more variously attested than the resurrection of Christ."[1]

The empty tomb

No one has ever found the body of Jesus.

He was laid to rest on the Friday evening in a new rock tomb belonging to a man named Joseph of Arimathea. His body had been wrapped round with long strips of linen inside which had been placed seventy-seven pounds of sweet-smelling ointments.

A large boulder had been rolled across the face of the tomb, closing up its entrance. It had been sealed on the express orders of the Roman governor, Pontius Pilate, after the Jewish authorities had asked him to authorize extra measures to ensure that no one would be able to tamper with the grave.

They knew that Jesus himself had predicted that he would rise again from the dead after three days, and they were concerned that his followers might attempt to steal the body and then claim that he had risen. As an additional precaution they obtained permission from Pilate to post a guard of soldiers to stand watch over the tomb. Their duty was to make certain that no one attempted to break into the grave. They knew that if they fell asleep on duty they would face death.

But on the Sunday morning the tomb was empty! John tells us in his Gospel account that when Mary of Magdala arrived at the tomb and found it so, she ran off to find Peter and John. "They have taken the Lord out of the tomb," she told them, "and we don't know where they have put him!" The men hurried to the tomb themselves and looked inside. What they saw were "the strips of linen lying there, as well as the burial cloth that had been around Jesus' head. The cloth was folded up by itself, separate from the linen" (John 20:6-7). What they saw caused them to believe.

How do we account for the evidence?

Was the body stolen?

What Peter and John saw when they entered the tomb made it obvious to them that no theft had taken place. A grave robber would not have left the burial clothes in the orderly state in which the disciples found them. Something more remarkable had taken place.

In any case it would have been almost impossible to steal the body, given the extra security measures that the authorities had taken. And the events of the following few weeks make this explanation even more unlikely.

If the religious leaders had stolen the body, they would only have needed to produce it in order to put the lid on Christianity for all time. After all, it was they who had worked for nearly three years to have Jesus silenced in the first place.

If the disciples had stolen the body, it would have been highly doubtful that they could have preached as they did. Right from the start their message was that Jesus Christ was alive. He'd been raised from the dead! From a physical point of view it would be highly unlikely that they could have done so if they knew exactly where his body was. Some of them were flogged, imprisoned, and even crucified for preaching what they would have known to be a lie.

One historian has written that the message about Jesus rising from the dead "could not have been maintained in Jerusalem for a single day, for a single hour, if the emptiness of the tomb had not been established as a fact."

The tomb was empty. And no one has ever found the body of Jesus Christ.

Did the early Christians make it all up?

This explanation is also highly unlikely. Many of the details in the accounts display what one writer has described as "a ring of truth" about them.

Take the discovery of the tomb, for example. All four Gospel writers tell us that it was the women friends of Jesus who found the empty tomb first (Matthew 28:1; Mark 16:1-3; Luke 24:1; John 20:1). You might pass over this piece of information, but by itself it is remarkable. A woman's evidence in a Jewish court of law was worth nothing. If you wanted people to believe a story that you'd made up you would not have included this information.

Then consider the appearances of Jesus after he died. How do we explain them? Over a period of forty days Jesus was seen by well over five hundred people. The New Testament records ten separate occasions, and there is a tremendous variety about them.

Mary met the risen Jesus in the graveyard itself when she came to embalm his dead body on the Sunday morning. Two of the disciples met him as they walked to the small village of Emmaus (about seven miles west of Jerusalem) on Sunday afternoon. He then appeared to a group of his disciples in the upstairs room of a house on Sunday evening. They thought they were looking at a ghost, but he told them, "Look at my hands and my feet. It is I myself! Touch me and see; a ghost does not have flesh and bones, as you see I have" (Luke 24:39).

Paul, writing to one church congregation, said that Jesus was seen by more than five hundred people on just one occasion. "Most of them are still alive," he said. So they could check it for themselves (1 Corinthians 15:6).

Was it a case of mass hallucination? Pinchas Lapide, a Jewish scholar, has recently investigated the events surrounding the resurrection. What particularly impressed him was the change in the disciples after it had happened. "No vision or hallucination," he said, "is sufficient to explain such a revolutionary transformation."

But what about Jesus Christ? The only possibility that really fits all the evidence is that Jesus was supernaturally raised from the dead that first Easter Sunday. Lapide's conclusion is this: "I accept the resurrection of Easter Sunday not as an invention of the community of disciples, but as a historical event."[2]

Life after death?

The writer and academic C.S. Lewis said that by rising from the dead, Jesus

> ... has forced open a door that had been locked since the death of the first man. He has met, fought and beaten the king of Death. Everything is different because he has done so. This is the beginning of the New Creation. A new chapter in cosmic history has opened.[3]

Because of the resurrection of Jesus we know that death is not the end. Jesus Christ proved it. He burst through the ultimate barrier. But he didn't do it for his own sake alone. He did it so that those who trust in him might also have safe passage and live their lives in the certainty of it.

Who will be your navigator through death? Jesus Christ is the only person in the history of the world who is qualified to be the guide.

Mohammed died at Mecca in 632 A.D. His body was cremated and his tomb is visited by thousands every year. No one claims that he rose from the dead.

The Buddha died at the age of eighty. His body was cremated and his ashes were distributed among eight groups of his followers who built shrines to put them in. No one claims that he rose from the dead.

But what about Jesus Christ?

I recently read the autobiography of David Watson, a gifted Christian teacher and preacher. As he lay awaiting death from cancer, he was able to write, "When I die, it is my firm conviction that I shall be more alive than ever, experiencing the full reality of all that God has prepared for us in Christ."[4]

If that is true, is there a more relevant message for our world than the resurrection of Jesus? Hope is in short supply these days. A politician once said, "You cannot live without hope any more than you can live without oxygen." By raising Jesus from the dead, God offers us solid hope.

I remember speaking to a woman called Mary who was close to death. "I can think of no greater privilege than this," she said, "that when I die I shall go to be with Jesus."

Is there life after death? Yes, if the resurrection is true.

The question of responsibility

Am I accountable for what I do in life? Do my actions have an eternal significance? If so, to whom am I responsible? Is it to myself, or to God? And will justice be done in the end—and be seen to be done? Most people want this to happen, but is there any guarantee?

Who's to judge?

We live in a world that has largely ignored or even rejected the idea that one day we will face God as judge. This is entirely understandable. For we have squeezed God himself out of life.

But is it wise? Have we enough evidence to do so confidently, and live as if we are responsible only to ourselves?

Writers like Alexander Solzhenitsyn have pointed clearly to the dangers of these attitudes in contemporary society.

When he received the Templeton Prize in 1983 he said in his acceptance speech:

> The entire twentieth century is being sucked into a vortex of atheism and self-destruction. We can only reach with determination for the warm hand of God, which we have so rashly and self-confidently pushed away . . . There is nothing else to cling to in the landslide.[5]

He was echoing the words of Jesus himself, for no one spoke more about the dangers of rejecting God than he did.

Jesus said that one day the world will be called to account. On that day a just "verdict" will be passed on the lives of each one of us. He said that the basis upon which that verdict will be decided will be our attitude toward him. If our lives have shown that we have acknowledged him as the Lord in his world then he will welcome us into eternity. But if we've shut him out of our lives, then our decision to do so will be confirmed forever.

Choices

Jesus spoke a lot about heaven. He made membership a free gift to all who would receive it. It is a place where he will reign forever. It will be populated by those who have accepted his invitation and sought to live under his authority. Justice, beauty, and all that is pure and good will be celebrated there forever.

But Jesus also spoke a great deal about hell. Imagine what it would be like to be cut off from every trace of goodness, beauty, and love, and you would be close to imagining the grim horror of what hell will be like. For that is what it means to be separated from God forever.

Jesus came to emphasize the choice we have. He commanded his disciples to alert the people to the seriousness of the situation.

The resurrection is the sign that this will take place. Paul says in the New Testament that the day is coming "when [God] will judge the world with justice by the man he has appointed. He has given proof of this to all men by raising him from the dead" (Acts 17:31).

Facing the issue
If it is true that one day I will stand before a perfect judge who will pass the verdict on my life, then the relevance of this fact to my own choices and attitudes in life is plain to see.

Most of all it must affect my attitude to Jesus Christ himself. If he *is* the supreme power in heaven and earth—as the New Testament says he is because of his resurrection—have I lived my life under his authority? That's the issue.

The question of life

A student once wrote, "People bustle and strive and hurry. Their eyes are mostly on material considerations. They die, and apparently it's all over. What are we here for anyway? There must be some purpose in living, but I haven't found it yet. I'm restless and unhappy."[6]

What is the purpose of life? Has it any real meaning? Or is the best plan to make the most of it and attempt to enjoy it while you can?

Most people seem content to live with the uncertainties and make the most of them. The guitarist Eric Clapton told *Tracks* magazine, "Life's like a razor blade, and I'll always walk along its edge."

Living in a new way
But if the resurrection of Jesus really took place, it unlocks uncertainties for the whole of life.

Look at the disciples of Jesus. By any reckoning the change in them after the resurrection is one of the most dramatic turn-arounds in history.

When Jesus was crucified their whole world caved in around them. Their leader had been crucified as a political threat to the established order. And they were caught up in it. Might not the authorities turn on them, too? Many of them simply ran away to avoid getting caught up in the backlash.

Then came the resurrection.

From a bunch of frightened cowards—like rabbits cornered in the blinding glare of a car's headlights—they are suddenly different. They possess new energy. Their preaching is dynamic. They're ready to face anybody and anything in their newly discovered cause. They believe that Jesus *is* alive!

What had changed them?

Right at the heart was the fact that they'd begun to realize who Jesus really was. They were coming to realize that in Jesus, God himself was at work in the world. He possessed the very key to life. He had demonstrated the ultimate authority over death. And through his resurrection he was offering them new hope and the reality of new life.

It was the knowledge of these certainties that changed the disciples. And it's these same certainties that are changing people today.

A *new dimension*

Tim was a person who literally stumbled upon Christianity. He was a drummer. This particular night he'd gone to the wrong hall expecting a band practice. Instead he found himself listening to a preacher telling about Jesus Christ. Somehow he was gripped by the message. "I don't know why I came," he said, "but God has really spoken to me tonight." He wrote to me later saying that his whole outlook on life had been completely changed by the truth he'd heard that night.

Jan had heard the message before but had never taken action. She found prayer difficult and often felt like there was no one there. She finally gave her life over to Jesus Christ during a church retreat weekend, and later she wrote that she would never have believed the difference that becoming a Christian would make. "I used to hope that God would listen to my prayers, but now I *know* that he does because I know the one I'm talking to."

Becoming a Christian, however, doesn't suddenly make life easy. We still come across the same problems. And we will have new problems to face as well. Jesus never promised his followers an easy life. Living under his direction will bring new challenges—both within ourselves and among other people. We will be operating under new orders in a world that won't understand. A friend of mine who works in a large city told me that being a Christian in that environment is sometimes like trying to fight your way up a "down" escalator during the peak rush-hour! But what we do have are new resources—the presence of God's Spirit within us—to help us to deal with the problems. As someone said to me recently, being a Christian is like "living life with an extra dimension."

■ In summary

If the resurrection of Jesus is true, then Christianity is supremely relevant—relevant to the question of death, relevant to the question of responsibility, relevant to the meaning of life. And it will remain relevant whether we choose to believe in it or not. It demands a response, for truth cannot change.

You may never have thought about the resurrection as being true before. Or perhaps you've thought it might be true but have never seen what follows from that truth. Don't put Christianity to one side and then forget about it. The issues are too important for that. They concern the meaning of life, death, and eternity.

What could be more relevant than that?

chapter

❸

"I've never really thought about it"

- "I'm too busy."
- "I've never really thought about it."
- "When I've got the time I'll give it some thought."

How often people say it. But time never comes as we'd like it to. And there are no signs that life is easing up. In most major cities, the peak of the busy rush-hour is nearly an hour earlier in the mornings and an hour later in the evenings than it was even ten years ago.

We live under pressure. No wonder one person said, "These days people just don't have the time."

That's certainly one side of the problem—and many people we surveyed talked about it. Perhaps for some there was the feeling that it was a waste of time looking into Christianity. Others admitted that they simply didn't know enough about it.

One student gave as her most important reason, "I have to admit that I do not know what Christianity *is*." Another said simply, "Ignorance."

Let me begin with a true story.

When I started junior high my parents gave me the chance to learn how to play a musical instrument. I'd been struggling to play the piano up to that point and felt that a new instrument might bring out the musical genius that, as an eleven-year-old, I knew was in me. The choice was easy. The only spaces left in the teaching timetable were for the classical guitar or the french horn. I started to learn the classical guitar.

A few years later I was invited to join a rather upper-crusty guitar club that met in oak-panelled rooms over tea on Sunday afternoons. Each week we would attempt to play duets by Bach, Corelli, or Telemann, and (after the cucumber sandwiches) one of us would give a small "concert" for the rest of the members. It was all very polite.

After a few months the inevitable happened. I'd been dreading it almost as soon as I'd joined: it was *my* turn.

To say that I was nervous would have been an understatement. I was so nervous that I managed to contract gastric flu, which meant that the very afternoon I was supposed to be performing Bach's lute suite in E minor, I was lying in bed, ill—but relieved!

When I arrived for my lesson the following week I learned the incredible news from my teacher, Mr. Higgins. "Segovia was at the guitar society on Sunday."

What!? I could hardly believe it. Andres Segovia, *the* most famous classical guitarist of all time! And I'd missed him. I still can't decide whether I'm disappointed that I wasn't there or relieved that I didn't get the chance to play in front of him.

But suppose that I had played. What would he have thought of my guitar playing? If he'd been honest he might (very understandably) have said that he was used to giving and hearing performances of the highest standard and that my playing was an embarrassment to him. He might, on the other hand, have covered up his true feelings and tried to encourage a youthful enthusiast with a long way to go. We shall never know.

But think of this story as a picture of something far more important.

Suppose that what we were saying about Christianity in chapter two is *true*. That one day we *will* stand before our Maker and that an exact and totally fair verdict will be given about our lives. If that is the case, would it not be vitally important to know what standard of human life we are going to be assessed by, and whether God will be strict or easy-going in his judgment?

So what should human life be like? And what is God like? The Bible is crystal clear on both points.

What does it mean to be "human"?

There is a great deal of confusion today about the question, "What does it really mean to be human?" History is littered with attempts to find the answer. Philosophers, song-writers, novelists, and playwrights have written millions of words on the subject. And yet something of a mystery still remains.

Shakespeare's King Lear said, "Who is it that can tell me who I am?" The rock band Supertramp summed up the search by recording "The Logical Song." The refrain goes:

Won't you please,
Please tell me what we've learned,
I know it sounds absurd,
But please tell me who I am.[1]

There are some who say that being human ultimately means nothing. Francis Bacon, the twentieth-century painter, wrote, "Man now realizes that he is an accident. He is a completely futile being and must play out the game without reason."

Many people secretly feel the same way but would not dare to put it into words. The very routine of daily life can

sometimes bring its own kind of meaninglessness. The
Police song "Synchronicity II" describes the urban rat race.

> Another working day has ended,
> Only the rush hour hell to face,
> Packed like lemmings into shiny metal boxes,
> Contestants in a suicidal race.[2]

But the "routine trap" is not confined to city workers
alone. Somebody once left a suicide note that said simply,
"I've just run out of things to do."

Yet for most people, to say that life is totally meaningless doesn't quite satisfy. There is much in our lives that
suggests there is some deeper meaning to it all. True,
we're not perfect, but there is much that is good within
human beings. We *are* capable of killing. But we're also
capable of great kindness. The mountaineer Chris
Bonington put it like this in a recent television interview:
"Man has got this capacity for unbelievable good and
unbelievable bad."

Others have come to a similar conclusion. Bob Geldoff
wrote in his autobiography: "It is the greatest failing of
humanity and at the same time the greatest attribute of
humanity that we constantly reach for things that exceed
our grasp."[3]

Blaise Pascal, the seventeenth-century French philosopher, wrote that human beings have tremendous potential but are never quite able to live up to it. In his book of
Thoughts he wrote:

> Man does not know the place he should occupy. He has
> obviously gone astray; he has fallen from his true place
> and cannot find it again. He searches everywhere,
> anxiously but in vain, in the midst of impenetrable
> darkness.[4]

How then does this all relate to the question of how God
will assess our lives? What will his reaction be? Will he

overlook the bad parts and commend us for the good? Or will he condemn us because the bad spoils the good?

The "hope it'll be all right" approach
"If God is really there he'll understand," some people say. "After all, he's a God of love . . . Anyway, I do my best. No one could ask for more."

But the Bible doesn't allow us to see things this way. In the first place it is uncompromising in its description of God's character. Yes, he *is* a God of love. The Bible frequently describes him as being "full of compassion and mercy" (e.g., James 5:11).

But he is also perfect. And he can accept us on no other grounds than that we are made perfect ourselves, not because he is trying to be awkward or make things difficult for us, but simply because he *is* perfection in himself. This is what the New Testament means when it says that "God is light; in him there is no darkness at all" (1 John 1:5). Light cannot mix with darkness. Where light exists there cannot be darkness. One cancels out the other. In the same way a perfect God cannot "mix" with those who fall short of this standard. So long as we are imperfect, we would never survive in his presence for a moment. We must become like light if we are to live in *his* light.

It is, therefore, foolish to base our lives on the hope that God might be different than what he actually is—that he will overlook our failures and still accept us. The character of God that is shown to us by Jesus and described by the Bible is unmistakable.

The "do-it-yourself" approach
We live in a "do-it-yourself" world. Within three miles of where I live you can visit four massive "Home and Garden" centers where you can get all you want for the odd jobs around the house.

So how about it? Shouldn't it be possible to become a better person by a "D.I.Y." approach—and perhaps eventually reach the standard that God requires?

Some thinkers have suggested that the human race is on the verge of dramatic improvement. In fact, for some optimists, the human race is to become the spearhead whereby the world is to become an altogether better place to live. Some years ago a few eminent scientists were invited to write articles for the *Sunday Times* on the topic "The Destiny of Man." What they wrote was later published in a book of the same name. One of the contributors, Julian Huxley (a famous zoologist), wrote confidently that human beings were on the way up. "Our immediate duty," he wrote, "is to spread and clarify the new key ideas about our evolutionary destiny, at the same time giving them practical application where possible." He went on to say that this was "the surest way to bring about world unity and to give modern man any real confidence about himself."

But for all its optimism, we would have to admit that the signs of this actually happening to the human race are pretty unpromising. "Civil Unrest Rocks Province"; "Peace Talks in Jeopardy"; "Man Jailed for Indecent Assault"; "30 Dead in Terrorist Bomb Outrage." These are the realities of the daily headlines. And will it ever be any different? The evidences suggests not.

And what about the individual? Is there any sign that we're able by ourselves to overcome those faults that we're conscious of?

What about New Year resolutions? How long does it take *you* to rip them up? Twenty-four hours? A couple of days?

There is something within us that stops us from making permanent improvement—let alone reaching perfection. Bertrand Russell, the atheist thinker, wrote that what stands in the way is "the evil passions in human minds: suspicion, fear, lust for power, intolerance."

In any case, if the "D.I.Y." approach were possible, how good would one have to be? A little better? Much better?

Once we start thinking about standards of human behavior, we quickly begin to compare ourselves with other people: "I may not be perfect, but I'm certainly better than *that* person," or "I've never done anything as bad as *that*."

But the Bible doesn't invite us to compare our lives with others around us. That would be to set up our own standards of what might or might not be acceptable. Instead, it is very clear about how human life is intended to be. And it doesn't spell it out in theory alone. It shows us someone who has actually achieved it in practice. If we're to succeed by the "D.I.Y." approach, then we must match up to *his* life.

The life of Jesus

In chapter one we saw that Jesus shows us what God is like. He was God in human form. But he also came to show us what true human life was intended to be like as well.

And what a life! There has never been another like it. The poet Tennyson wrote that Jesus' character was "more wonderful than the greatest miracle." Mahatma Gandhi looked at Jesus' life and said, *"That* is how human life ought to be lived."

Someone has said that Jesus combined those qualities that we would most like to possess in our best moments. He was a person of deep compassion and love. He cared for ordinary people in all the trials and pressures of life. His heart was drawn to those who were suffering, and he loved to spend time with those who were cast aside by society. He was no simple "gentle Jesus, meek and mild" as the line in the children's hymn goes. He had the strongest sense of what was right and just. And he was never afraid to stand up for it—whatever the consequences.

But he never overstepped the mark. No one could ever accuse him of doing anything wrong. On one occasion he challenged his hearers to do so but they simply couldn't fault him. And Peter—one of his closest friends, who spent just about every waking hour in his immediate company for nearly three years—was later to describe his character like this:

He committed no sin, and no one ever heard a lie come from his lips. When he was insulted, he did not answer

back with an insult; when he suffered, he did not
threaten. *1 Peter 2:22-23, Good News Bible*

Reactions

How did people respond to Jesus?

His life provoked the strongest reactions, at both ends of
the spectrum. Many were drawn irresistibly to him. His
mastery of life marked him out as unique—like listening
to a live performance after hearing countless scratched old
records. So much so that the gospel accounts record that
he was followed by large crowds wherever he went.

Others were made to feel very uncomfortable with him
around. His standards were uncompromising, and he expected the highest in others, too, particularly those in
authority. Like the most expensive record stylus he brought
out the best in others but also made their "scratches" very
clear.

People don't like being shown up. Plato, the Greek philosopher who lived four hundred years before Jesus, had
predicted what people would do to the "perfect" human
being. He "will be scourged, tortured and imprisoned . . .
and after enduring every humiliation he will be crucified"
(Republic, 361, 364).

And that's exactly what happened to Jesus. The religious
leaders cooked up false charges against him. Luke tells us
in his Gospel that Pontius Pilate, the Roman governor,
declared three times that he could find nothing in Jesus
that he could fault (Luke 23:4, 14, 22).

But Pilate eventually handed Jesus over to them to do
as they wanted. He agreed to release Barabbas, a convicted
criminal who was to have been crucified, and allowed Jesus
to be crucified in his place, innocent though he was. And as
the soldiers hammered the nails into his hands and feet he
prayed for his accusers, "Father, forgive them, for they do
not know what they are doing" (Luke 23:34). Then as he
hung on the cross, one of the two convicted criminals
crucified on either side of him said, "We are punished justly,

for we are getting what our deeds deserve. But this man has done nothing wrong" (Luke 23:41). Even the Roman centurion in charge of his crucifixion said, "Surely this was a righteous man" (Luke 23:47).

God's "blueprint"

The Bible describes Jesus as God's "blueprint" for humanity, his last word on what it means to be truly human. And the lives of human beings were designed to reflect what he perfectly demonstrated.

For you and I were created in God's image, says the Bible (Genesis 1:27). We were designed to live in obedient harmony with God—that's how we were to get the best out of life. But we have pushed God out of the picture, have rejected his intention for our lives, and live as if he didn't exist. As a result the "image" has become spoiled. We don't match the designer's plans. Our lives are not what they should be. We still carry a "reflection" of God's character. We still carry a vague idea of what might have been had we the ability to achieve it. But the real thing is to be found only in the person of Jesus. Here alone was a man who lived his life in total obedience to the will of God. And he said repeatedly that to live in this way brought him the greatest fulfillment of all. It's the purpose for which you and I were created, but it is only in Jesus that we find it perfectly demonstrated.

So, if we want to see how human life was intended to be lived, then we are to look at *his* life.

But while it's true that most people would agree with Napoleon that "between Jesus and whomsoever else in the world there is no comparison," few take to heart what follows on from it. For if the standard of Jesus' life is the only one that is acceptable to a perfect God, then it is by *this* standard that you and I will be assessed on the day when we stand before God. Our lives will be measured against *his*.

Falling short

If we're honest, most of us struggle with *our own* standards, let alone *his*. But what if we are compared to Jesus? As one student said to me, *"No one* has lived like him."

The Bible simply and clearly confirms what we know in our hearts if we're honest. If this is the standard, then we've fallen far short. We've missed the mark.

The word "sin" is a small but devastating word that is much misunderstood by people today. Keith Richards of the Rolling Stones said, "There are very few things, apart from genocide and a few other major things like that, that I would say are actually wrong." But the Bible's meaning of the word "sin" is much deeper than that. It is the extent to which our lives fall short of the human life of Jesus. And when you realize *that*, it is immediately clear that not one of us is excluded from this word "sin." As the apostle Paul wrote in the New Testament, "All have sinned and fall short of the glory of God" (Romans 3:23).

Right with God?

How then can anyone be fit for God's presence? And how do Christians claim that God accepts them—that he has forgiven them and now treats them as his friends?

So far the news has not been encouraging. Jesus alone has met God's standard. He alone has qualified for heaven and has left us an example that we will never be able to match—like canoes being jostled in the wake of a power boat! So where's the good news? For Christianity *is* good news.

The heart of it is this: Jesus came into our world, not only to show us what a perfect life is like, but also to do something about the fact that our own lives do not match up to the standard God requires. He did it by making it possible for us to share in *his* perfection so that we might be fully acceptable to God. And by doing so he made it possible for us to begin to rediscover the reason why we were created— that we might be united with the Creator and fulfill God's purpose for us.

And he achieved all this through his death.

More than a third of the gospel accounts in the New Testament are about the death of Jesus and what it means. It is absolutely central to Christianity. "If you want to understand the Christian message," said Martin Luther (the great sixteenth-century church reformer), "you must start with the wounds of Jesus."

Jesus himself repeatedly talked about his coming death as something to which the whole of his life was leading. He said again and again that this was the very reason he had come into the world (see, for example, the statements recorded in Mark's Gospel—8:31; 9:31; 10:33).

What did his death achieve?

We said at the start of this chapter that God is both perfect *and* full of mercy—and it is both these sides of his character that find their fullest expression in the death of Jesus.

The writers of the Bible describe what his death means with many different pictures, but all of them illustrate the same truth—that when Jesus died on the cross he was dying in *my* place. He was doing something for me that I could never do for myself. Peter describes it in this way: "For Christ died for sins once for all, the righteous for the unrighteous, to bring you to God" (1 Peter 3:18).

When Jesus died, he died as a perfect person, willingly taking the punishment that sinners deserve. He did it for you, and he did it for me.

Imagine a judge who, after weighing the evidence brought forward against the offender, proceeds to announce the inescapable verdict of "Guilty!" He can do nothing else. The offender stands convicted by the due process of law. But then imagine that this same judge halts the proceedings, walks over to the guilty party, takes his place in the dock, and offers to pay the penalty himself. What happens to the offender? He is still guilty, but the judge has stood in to pay the penalty on his behalf. The guilty person is therefore free.

This picture illustrates the heart of what God did through the death of Jesus. The inevitable verdict on our

lives on the last day will be "Guilty!" for we've all failed to
reach the required standard. But God himself has acted on
our behalf. In his astonishing love and mercy he has come
to us in the person of Jesus, has shown us what the verdict
will be—ahead of time—and has made it possible through
the death of Jesus for that verdict to be reversed. It is not
because we deserve it. It is not because our lives demonstrate that we are *actually* innocent. Quite the opposite
is true. It is only because the one who stands in our
place—Jesus himself—is innocent. And *his* innocence, the
perfection of *his* life, is "credited to our account" so that we
can be acceptable to God. The apostle Paul summed it up
when he said that "In *Jesus* we can be made right with God"
(2 Corinthians 5:21, my translation).

As a result, anyone who comes to God with genuine
sorrow for past failure, and a genuine desire to live as God
wants, can be truly forgiven because of the death of Jesus.

This is what Christianity is all about. This is the news
that Christians get excited about. Because of the death of
Jesus, whenever God looks at a Christian believer he sees
Jesus Christ. He no longer sees a deeply flawed life. He sees
the faultless life of his son. Impossible? Someone said to me
after I'd explained it to him, "This sounds too good to be
true." But it isn't. If you can understand this, you've understood the heart of Christianity.

Of course, this will mean radical changes in my life. I
cannot remain the same kind of person after I've received
God's forgiveness. From that moment on he demands that
my life should conform more and more to the pattern that
Jesus shows me. But at the heart of Christianity is the fact
that God accepts me not because I am a good person—or
am trying to be one—but because Jesus died in my place.

A perfect life?

What do you see when you look at your life? And how does
it compare to that of Jesus Christ?

And what does *God* see when he looks at your life? Does he see you as you actually are? Or does he see the perfect life of Jesus Christ because you've received pardon through his death?

One person described the discovery of what it means to know God's pardon in this way: "It's like a great burden rolling off my shoulders." And many millions have made the same discovery.

■ In summary

Many people have never taken the time to think about whether their lives match the standard that God requires. If this is true of you, isn't it time that you started examining the accounts of Jesus? For in the life of Jesus alone do we see God's standards fully demonstrated. And only through his death may we be put right with God, be ready for his verdict, and begin to live as we ought.

So if these things are true, shouldn't you act on them? It will be the most important thing you've ever done.

chapter

④

"The biggest obstacle is the church"

All in all, the organized church took a beating in our survey. The responses showed that many felt the church was bad advertising for Christianity. Many saw it as the biggest obstacle preventing them from believing.

One thirty-year-old woman summed up her opinion: "The church is a bit of a joke!" A college student complained that it "is outdated and irrelevant." Others said it's "full of 'old cronies' and archaic values"; "It's reactionary."

And what of its activities? "Services are irrelevant!" "They're boring!"

Most seriously, many felt that something was wrong within the church itself. It had drifted. It no longer stood for the truth. One person expressed it like this: "The church as an institution lacks Christianity."

It projects a money-grabbing image. It has become obsessed with keeping itself going and seems unconcerned about the world out there with all its problems.

Then there's the hypocrisy: "I became disillusioned with Christianity after many years of church attendance. I did not see many Christians (including the clergy) who actually followed the word of Christ."

A policewoman said, "It's the hypocrisy of the church that pushes me away from practicing religion in a formal way."

"The church is dead!"

You might get the impression from many church buildings that the whole idea of Christianity has had its day. It has served its purpose, but it's best to forget about it now. The popular image doesn't help: the television evangelist, the church with the thermometer outside saying how much (or how little) has been raised to keep the steeple up.

All this is true. The church often looks more dead than alive, as if it were being propped up until finally laid to rest. But is it wise to reject the whole of Christianity because some churches are dead?

Let's face it. Some churches *are* dead! But you should no more judge Christianity on this basis than you should imagine that because one cinema has been turned into a bingo hall, the film industry is dead!

The theologian Karl Barth said, "If we wish to hear the call of Jesus, we must hear it despite the church." That is often sadly true.

Jesus himself spoke in plain words about churches like these. The book of Revelation (the last book in the Bible) is full of warnings about what happens to churches that abandon the truth about God and fail to demonstrate his love. God will withdraw from them.

Some churches become lukewarm in their love for God. Some allow lies to infiltrate and turn people away from the true God. Yet others permit corruption to enter in. Jesus said it would happen. But that doesn't mean we should throw the whole idea of Christianity out.

So thank God this isn't the whole story. For every dead church you take me to, I could take you to many that are alive with the reality of the living God. Places where God's truth is taught from the Bible. Places where the Spirit of God is active, helping people to understand what the truth about God means in their everyday lives, and enabling them to love each other as they themselves receive God's love. Places where people are finding the living God.

Is the church dying?

Not at all! In fact, on a worldwide scale it is growing faster than ever before.

Take Korea as an example. At the turn of the century, there were around 42,000 Christians. By the mid-1980s this number had increased to 11½ *million* (around 30 percent of the population). It is not unknown to come across churches where more people attend services on a Sunday than attend the Superbowl in the United States. One congregation has a membership of half a million.

Or take India. A recent research project by the Church Growth Research Center in Madras has calculated that the number of adult Christians in India has doubled in the last two decades (from 9¾ million in 1970 to almost 19 million in 1989).

In Africa and South America the church is experiencing growth, too. For example, the church in Kenya has grown from 5,000 in 1900 to 8 million in 1975.

Though one must be careful about the kinds of conclusions drawn from statistics, they do at least show a steady growth in the number of Christians worldwide. It is impossible to argue, therefore, that the church is on the way out. The evidence points in the opposite direction. Hundreds of millions of people in the world today claim that Jesus Christ is alive. New churches are being planted every day.

The church is irrelevant

Is the established church irrelevant to you? Sadly, it is for many. Some religious leaders do seem to be more concerned with buildings than with people.

It's even more tragic when you consider that people generally have not lost the basic instinct that "God" (in some shape or form) does exist. A recent MORI poll found that among 18-30-year-olds, 64 percent still held to some belief in "God." But it is obvious that the vast majority of these people don't feel that what the church has to say is relevant to these instinctive beliefs or that it will help them to discover who this "God" really is. Look at the number who actually go to church. Attendance in Britain, for example, has slipped from 35 percent of the population in 1900 to just 11% in 1986.

The early church

By contrast, the church life of the earliest believers, described in the New Testament, was anything but irrelevant. Of course, there were no buildings. No one thought anything about building churches until many years later. The church, then as now, is people—not the building. They simply met in each other's homes.

People look back at this church as the golden era. "Why can't the church be like this again?" Well, of course it wasn't all perfect. Far from it. The church has always had a membership made up entirely of sinners. And the early church was no exception. If you read the story in the New Testament you'll see it had its own share of problems.

But even so, the early Christians (the "church" of the day) showed qualities that every "live" church will possess in some measure.

They were "different"

Something had happened to these early Christians. You could pick them out in a crowd. On their first public appearance they seemed intoxicated and drunk. At least that's what some bystanders said. They spoke with authority, and they pointed to the resurrection of Jesus, even though most of the crowd had seen him put to death.

Were they mad? Not at all. Peter, the leader, pointed to the power that has marked every true group of believers ever since: the living power of God's Spirit. It was he who had set them on fire, and he has been doing so ever since.

Have you ever been impressed by the lives of Christians? It's a fact that most people are drawn to Jesus Christ by the lives of their friends. Someone said to me recently that what first made him think about Christianity was the experience of going to a church where people were different. "They had something. And I wanted to know what it was."

Of course, the "superior" Christian is a real turn-off—the person who wants to give you the impression that he or she is somehow nearer to God, a "better" person than you are.

But people like this haven't really understood what being a Christian is. It is not a question of being better than someone else. A Christian is simply someone who has found forgiveness from God and wants others to find it, too. We're all on level ground. So it's like "one beggar telling another beggar where to find bread." And people who've really discovered God's forgiveness will always be aware of their own unworthiness.

But there was another thing about those early Christians.

They cared

A historian of the period has described their community life as "a society of love and mutual care which astonished the pagans and was recognized as something entirely new."

Not surprisingly, it made an impact. For here was a group of believers who believed things that really made a difference in the way they lived—no "Sundays only" religion here! Christianity should transform the whole of life. After all, it's about a whole new way of living. And that new life should be seen by others. Jesus himself said you can tell who the true Christians are by the "fruit" that their lives produce. If there's no fruit, or if the fruit is bad, then there must be something wrong with the tree itself. In the same way it may be that someone who is claiming to be a Christian, but whose life says something else, is not a true Christian after all.

Then there's a third thing that distinguished the early Christians.

They were full of joy
One person we talked to describes his reaction to "church" like this:

> The services are out of date and need to be more in keeping with the black gospel approach to religion . . . so that everyone can enjoy, understand, and feel part of what is going on, to feel revitalized, ready to cope with whatever life throws at you.

Many young people feel the same way.

There was certainly a reality about the early Christian meetings. They were marked with joy at sharing God's great blessings. They met together "with glad and sincere hearts, praising God and enjoying the favor of all the people" (Acts 2:46-47).

But it went along with a complete certainty that God himself was present in person, by his Spirit, whenever they met together. Sometimes he made his presence felt very powerfully. On one occasion Luke tells us that "after they prayed, the place where they were meeting was shaken. And they were all filled with the Holy Spirit and spoke the word of God boldly" (Acts 4:31).

At other times he worked more quietly. But *he* was the one who was always directing them. Helping them to focus on the truth about Jesus from the Scriptures. Helping them to pray. Giving them courage to speak for Jesus Christ. Revitalizing them and sending them out ready for anything. He was the one who gave them peace, love, and joy.

Quite a difference from some church services today!

But God is the same God. And churches across the world are rediscovering this joy and expressing it when they meet together. They are finding the same strength and power, too, to live for Jesus Christ and to tell others about him.

They broke social barriers

There's something very impressive about the make-up of the early church. There was a solidarity about it. It broke down barriers, both cultural and class.

But perhaps the most impressive of all was the demolition of the racial barrier. Non-Jews were being welcomed into the church. One historian of the period wrote, "No more deeply rooted racial prejudice . . . existed than Jewish prejudice against non-Jews." But even this wall was being breached. The early believers came to realize that, because of Jesus Christ, what united them was far greater than what kept them apart. Through his death, God was saying that their sins could be freely forgiven. A new start was possible. So if God was offering this forgiveness to Jews *and* non-Jews, who were they to refuse it to one another?

The good news of Jesus Christ restores relationships. At its heart is a new relationship with God; we become his children. But from this must flow new relationships with others, too—with believers of every shade and background. For when God accepts another person because he or she trusts in his Son, Jesus Christ, then I must accept that person, too, and welcome him or her as a new brother or sister.

The church is a sign that a new world is coming. Barriers of class and culture are being broken down.

No wonder that people sat up and took notice. There are churches today that urgently need to recapture these qualities. But don't be put off by the churches that seem "dead." For there are many other churches that are alive with the reality of the living God. They are places where God's truth is taught from the Bible, where God's joy is experienced, where practical care is put into action, and where true unity is found.

Look around and find one.

"The church is full of hypocrites!"

"Christians are the biggest obstacle," said one person we talked to. "They're all hypocrites!"

Hypocrisy is sickening. "It is the loudest lie," says one writer. And among religious people it is particularly obnoxious. For "to profess to love God while leading an unholy life," said Saint Augustine, "is the worst of all falsehoods."

There are at least two things to say about hypocrisy.

Jesus attacked it
If you are sick of hypocrites, so was Jesus.

He had no time for them. In fact, some of the strongest things he ever said were to the religious phonies of his day. Read Matthew's Gospel, chapter 23, verses 13-32 for his reactions. Hypocrites prevent people from coming to know God. Their lives are like walking lies. They say one thing and do another. No wonder Jesus was angry about them.

For one thing, hypocrites claim to be better than others. One young doctor in our survey described the type he'd met. They seemed to be "placing themselves above other men," he said, "saying they are somehow closer to God."

But that's not true Christianity. That's exactly what Jesus attacked in the hypocrites of his day. If people act like that, it's a sure sign they haven't yet discovered what real Christianity is about. They draw attention to themselves. They seem to be saying, "Look what I do. Aren't I good?"

But real Christians can never boast about themselves. To be a Christian is to be conscious of God's mercy. God doesn't accept some people because they're "better" than others. A Christian is simply somebody who has discovered that God can accept him (however good or bad he may be) only because of what Jesus Christ did for him on the cross.

It doesn't affect the truth of the Christian message

Just because some Christians put you off (for whatever reason), it doesn't mean that the message of Christianity itself is untrue.

Think of it this way. Christians are supposed to be signposts to the truth. This is one of the ways Jesus described his followers. Their lives were to point others to the reality of God and the truth about Jesus Christ.

Imagine that you are driving to a small country town called Scobey. You've never been there before so you're watching carefully for signs along the way. You come across a junction with a broken signpost. The name of the place you're looking for has been lost. You don't know which way to go.

What would your reaction be? Well, the last thing you'd think would be, "Ah, that means Scobey has ceased to exist." This wouldn't follow at all. On the other hand, you might well be thinking, "What a useless signpost! They ought to replace it with a better one."

At the end of the day you'll take longer to get to Scobey. But a broken signpost doesn't mean that the town itself doesn't exist. Sooner or later you'll come across a clearer one and be able to find your way.

■ In summary

You may have come across some Christians who are bad signposts. They haven't been very effective at pointing you in the right direction. They may even have put you off the track completely. But please don't decide on this basis that God, therefore, doesn't exist or that Christianity isn't true.

chapter

⑤

"There's so much suffering in the world"

- "There's too much suffering, too many wars, too many starving people, and too many evil people in the world to believe that we all come from one good and almighty creator in heaven."
- "I can't believe in Christianity because so many bad things have happened to me."
- "If God loves everybody, why does he allow so much violence and world suffering?"

Many express similar feelings. The fact of suffering faces us with real questions.

First of all, it seems to call into question whether God exists at all. A student psychiatric nurse put it this way: "I find it difficult to believe that if God did exist he'd allow starvation, illness, and all the other bad things in the world."

But if it is possible that God *does* exist, can we still believe in the loving God the Bible describes when the world we see around us is full of suffering?

There can be no one who has not thought about the agony of suffering in our world. For some it is a deeply personal question: "Why does God allow this to happen to me?" For others it raises intellectual questions about the suffering of others. For many people today its existence seems to make true happiness almost an impossible dream. As the actress Lauren Bacall said in an interview, "I don't see how anyone can be happy today except a newborn baby. Once you start reading newspapers you realize what a nightmare it all is."

Is God *really* there? And if he is, is he some kind of cosmic tyrant, enjoying our pain? A Depeche Mode song puts it like this:

> I don't want to start
> Any blasphemous rumors
> But I think that God's
> Got a sick sense of humor
> And when I die
> I expect to find him laughing.[1]

For many, then, suffering is the biggest obstacle to belief in God. The novelist Somerset Maugham wrote, "I'm glad I don't believe in God. When I look at the misery of the world and its bitterness I think that no belief can be more ignoble."

So are there any answers? Can we continue to believe in any sort of God these days? After Hitler and Hiroshima? After the Holocaust?

No "slick" solutions

I confess that I find the problem of suffering the hardest question of all to answer. The existence of suffering will always be partly mysterious. Our limited minds will never be able to understand fully why it is or what it might mean. So we should be wary about easy answers.

But I'm convinced that it is only as we hold on to the God of love whom Jesus Christ came to show us that we can attempt to make any sense of the suffering in our world, or begin to bring hope to those who are actually experiencing suffering.

Helmut Thielicke was a German theology professor who preached to thousands during lunch hour services in Stuttgart toward the end of the Second World War—even as Allied bombs were falling on the city.

He said that, as a Christian, looking at the problem of suffering was a bit like looking at a piece of woven cloth through a magnifying glass. As you look at any part of it, the center of the picture is in clear focus, made larger and clearer by the glass itself, but the edges appear to be blurred. The total picture is not clear.

In the same way, when we look at the problem of suffering and the existence of evil in the world, much of the picture remains unclear. Perhaps only one part of it is in focus, or ever will be.

Yet, for the Christian, the parts of the picture that *are* in clear focus can begin to make sense of the questions that still remain. The coming of Jesus into our world—his life, death, and resurrection—is like the center of the picture. And the Bible is like the magnifying glass. It brings into focus for us what these historical events really mean so that we can start to understand the wider picture. For many who are actually suffering it is these central facts that have brought hope and courage to hold on, to endure, to keep going.

What, then, can we say about suffering? Which questions does the Bible answer most clearly?

God did not create suffering

We must begin by saying that the world God made was perfect in every detail. The human race lived in perfect harmony with both Creator and creation. Just as it was meant to be.

But then came the rebellion. God had given us the ability to choose between right and wrong, between good and evil. He intended that we should have freedom of choice, and that we should exercise that freedom responsibly. We were not designed as robots, programmed to make right responses like a set of computerized machines. Robots can neither give nor receive love, nor can they make real choices. It would have been meaningless.

God wanted us to exercise the gift of free choice by responding to his love and by being his friends. That way we would discover the greatest good imaginable: Creator and creature in perfect harmony.

We used it instead to reject him from our lives and live in his world as if he didn't exist. Catastrophe followed.

Two catastrophes, in fact. First, that unique friendship with God was ended as we turned in on ourselves and began to chase after our own desires. Second, our harmony with the environment was also shattered as the created order itself felt the effect of that first rebellion.

This biblical explanation of *why* we are as we are is repeated again and again by its various writers. We have become enemies of God, and our environment has been mysteriously caught up in the fighting.

This helps to explain certain things that we see around us.

The result of human greed

Jesus himself said that the evils in our society originate not from God but from the hearts and minds of human beings. "For from the inside, from a person's heart, come the evil ideas which lead him to do immoral things, to rob, kill, commit adultery, be greedy, and do all sorts of evil things" (Mark 7:21-22, Good News Bible).

Isn't that true? Think of wars. Think of the greed that causes them. Think of the untold grief and horror. The senseless slaughter. Think of families and countries torn apart by rival armies.

But why do wars start? The Constitution of UNESCO,[2] at the United Nations, states: "Since wars begin in the minds of men, it is in the minds of men that the defense of peace must be constructed."

Or take the distribution of the world's resources. Recent estimates put the number of undernourished in the world at 500 million. 10,000 die of starvation each week. That's more than one every minute.

And yet it's a fact that there is enough food in the world to feed everyone.

How do we explain these statistics? We live in an age in which one quarter of the world has four-fifths of its wealth. But more importantly, we live in a world where people who possess wealth don't like giving it up. As Gandhi said, "There is a sufficiency in the world for man's need but not for man's greed."

It's easy to point the finger. But think about it. A photograph projected on a big screen is magnified from a very small slide. We would all admit there are huge problems in the world today. They are projected into our living rooms every evening. But many of them, says Jesus, are a projection of our own hearts.

Ian Charleson played the athlete Eric Liddell in the film *Chariots of Fire.* In order to prepare for the role he decided to study the Bible so that he could understand how Liddell might have reacted as a Christian. He describes what he found: "I learnt a lot from the man . . . You can't read the Bible with the kind of care I did without learning something yourself. I don't know if I believe in a supreme God the way Eric did, but it makes a lot of sense."

Charleson said that he stopped at the words of Jesus "from a person's heart came the evil ideas which lead him to do immoral things." "That really made me think," he explained. "Something like that strikes a chord in me because I know it's true."[3]

Have you ever thought, "Why doesn't God do something about it?" "Why doesn't he just wipe out evil at a stroke?"

He certainly could. But suppose for a moment that he actually *did*, say at midnight tonight. Would *you* be alive five minutes later? Would I? If he's going to wipe out every trace of evil then in all honesty we have to admit that he'd have to deal with us, too.

But what about earthquakes? What about tidal waves? What about natural disasters? Can we begin to make sense of these?

Here the Bible offers pointers rather than answers, but what we are told is that these, too, have a connection with human evil.

Human beings and the world in which they live are linked together in the Bible. They're all of a single piece. What happens to one inevitably affects the other, sooner or later. The present-day revival of interest and concern for environmental issues has emphasized this link very clearly. There's a chain-link effect in operation, like when you knock down the first in a row of dominoes and the others follow in order.

In the same way, when humans rebelled against their Creator, the created order itself was thrown out of joint. Consequently, it is also spoiled. It bears the hallmarks of its Creator—beauty, order, and goodness—but it also bears marks of something more sinister—pollution, decay, and disintegration. Like the creature, creation itself must also be restored.

God has defeated suffering

William Temple, archbishop of Canterbury during the Second World War, wrote these words:

> "There cannot be a God of love," men say, "because if there was, and he looked upon the world, his heart would break." The Church points to the Cross and says, "It did break." "It is God who made the world," men say. "It is he who should bear the load." The Church points to the Cross and says, "He did bear it."

The death of Jesus is the clearest proof of God's love for a suffering world. God is not a disinterested observer looking in from the outside—as some would have it. Far from it. He entered our world in the person of Jesus Christ and became subject to its pain and injustice. He knew hunger and thirst. He knew rejection and betrayal. He knew torture and the excruciating pain of crucifixion. He knew what it meant to be totally alone. And he knew death.

He became subject to human suffering, but as he died on the cross he broke its ultimate power.

One of the ways the Bible describes the death of Jesus is as a victory over the forces of evil. They threw everything they could at him but he still emerged the outright winner. The proof of this is that he rose from the dead. He had suffered the pain and horror of death by crucifixion but had been raised to new life.

"But why is there still suffering and evil in the world if Jesus has already defeated it?"

Perhaps an illustration may help. Imagine a game of chess being played by two international "Masters." I happened to be watching a game like this on the television recently when one of the players suddenly resigned. Just before he did so, I, like he, had been surveying his options. He didn't seem to be under any direct threat. He certainly wasn't "in check." And yet he still resigned. Why?

In the interview afterward, he explained that he'd just seen his opponent make a move that would sooner or later bring him certain victory, so there was no real point in playing on.

Now imagine you or I were playing against this chess "Master." We probably wouldn't realize that the decisive move had been played. We would probably play on. Move a pawn. Reposition the castle. Move the king one square. But in reality the game is already over. It's only a matter of time. The result is a certainty. We've lost.

The Bible says that the death and resurrection of Jesus are like that decisive move in the cosmic struggle against evil and all its consequences. The victory is ultimately

certain but the opposition is playing on. The evidence of the
battle is still around us. But the final result is certain. And
one day the victory will be plain for all to see.

God can use suffering as a warning

C.S. Lewis wrote, "God whispers to us in our pleasures,
speaks in our conscience, but shouts in our pains: it is his
megaphone to rouse a deaf world."

Suffering shouts at us. "Why should these things happen?" "It's unfair." "Why me?"

Perhaps most of all it cries out that all is not well with
the world. It reminds us—if we're willing to listen—that
we're creatures in a universe that is suffering from decay.
And this decay is terminal—as we ourselves are.

What then should we do? What questions ought we to be
asking ourselves?

Jesus himself was once asked about a disaster in which
a tower collapsed, killing eighteen people. The natural
question arose, "Why does God allow it?" But Jesus didn't
get involved in a discussion about why God might have
allowed it, or whether it was a just punishment or not.
What he said was simply, "Unless you repent, you too will
all perish" (Luke 13:5).

Jesus brings the issue into sharp focus. Death will one
day claim each one of us one way or another. The collapse
of the tower was so sudden that no one had time to prepare
for it. So Jesus says that each one of us must be reconciled
to God while we still have time. *Then* may be too late.

Often I hear people say, "Maybe later in life I'll think
about Jesus Christ. When I've got more time." But listen
to the words of Jesus. We live in a world of uncertainty. You
may not have that time. Are you right with God?

God can transform suffering

Often the greatest saints this world has seen are those who
have suffered the most. God doesn't always take us out of

the path of suffering, but he will help us to bear it. As Paul Tournier, the Swiss psychologist, wrote, "It is in suffering that I perceive Christ's nearness, his presence, and his participation in life."

I remember a young woman called Liz coming to see me during a week of meetings about Christianity that I was leading at the teacher training college. The first thing that struck me about her was her expression. She wore the look of someone who had been through a great deal. Her story spilled out as we talked. She had once called herself a Christian but had turned her back on God. She had suffered much herself and had caused suffering to others, too. She couldn't believe that God could forgive her or that he cared about what had happened. Her heart had become hard, and she was full of bitterness.

I tried to explain to her that God had not abandoned her. That Jesus demonstrated by his own death that he was able to identify completely with those who are suffering, whatever its cause might be.

We talked for some time before she finally got up to leave, saying she might come back the following day.

Some hours later, as she later told me, she found herself sitting in somebody's front garden. She had no idea how she got there, but as she cried out to God in anger she became aware that Jesus himself was with her, right alongside her. It was not only that he sympathized with her—though that was certainly a great comfort. She came to realize for herself what his death had actually accomplished. It meant she could be free from the burden of hopelessness that had overwhelmed her. It meant that she could load her bitterness onto another. That burden had been taken by him, and she could lift her head again, for the first time in years. She began to experience hope and joy at her discovery.

The following day she was a completely transformed person. Her face told a different story. Her eyes were radiant. She was full of life. It was difficult to believe that this was the same person.

God never abandons us in our suffering. The death of Jesus on the cross is the ultimate, down-to-earth proof of this. It stands true for all time. And because Jesus knows what it is to suffer he's present with us when we suffer.

His selflessness as he died has also proved a powerful example to those who suffer unjustly for their faith. Many of the New Testament letters were written to people who were being persecuted for their Christian beliefs. Those who wrote to them often sought to encourage them by calling to mind the example of Jesus, whose love for his persecutors remained stronger than their hatred.

In our own day, Irina Ratushinskaya, the Russian poetess, imprisoned in a labor camp for her faith, said, "I can testify that only those who do not hate their torturers are not broken by them."

God will unveil a new world

But there is a final reason why God can bring hope even in the jaws of suffering. God is going to recreate this world, and it will be perfect.

The Bible contains many pictures of it; perhaps the most famous is in the last book—the book of Revelation. "He will wipe every tear from their eyes. There will be no more death or mourning or crying or pain, for the old order of things has passed away" (Revelation 21:4).

When you read the gospel accounts of Jesus' life you catch glimpses of what this new world will be like. Many of his miracles put right what had gone wrong in the world. The lame were made to walk; the deaf were made able to hear; the dead were raised to life; the storm on the lake was stilled. These were signs, pointing to a new world yet to come. Creation was being put back together, it was being restored to its proper order.

It's a bit like seeing a preview at the cinema before the main feature film. Across the screen flashes the message "For Future Presentation." Then comes a clip from a film to be shown in the near future. All you get is a taste of it.

A couple of minutes maybe. But enough to whet the appetite. It makes you want to come back to experience the real thing.

Jesus' miracles are something like this. They give us a glimpse of what this new world will be like. And they point to Jesus himself, who will bring it into being.

It's the certainty of this future world for those who trust in Jesus that has kept Christians together even in the middle of appalling suffering. St. Paul, who suffered more than most, was able to write, "I consider that our present sufferings are not worth comparing with the glory that will be revealed in us" (Romans 8:18).

Mikhail Khorev, a Baptist pastor in Russia, was imprisoned for six years because of his Christian faith. During that time he wrote,

> When I am walking round the exercise yard, I like to go over all the mercies for which I must thank the Lord ... I haven't enough fingers to count them all on. In Life Eternal, the value of suffering for Christ will be even more clearly revealed to me, and I will give thanks to the Lord again and again. Here, not everything can be understood, but there all will become clear.[4]

That final sentence reminds us of the cloth and the magnifying glass with which we began this chapter. Here is someone who is able to endure suffering because Jesus Christ has made the center of the picture clear.

■ In summary

Can we still believe in a loving God when the world is suffering?

There will always remain unanswered questions. But I've tried to show that we really can only begin to make sense of the problems of suffering as we allow the Bible to bring the center of the picture into focus. It points to the truth that human beings are involved in the sorry mess of a world at odds with its Maker. But it emphasizes above all God's intervention in Jesus Christ. He came into a suffering world because of God's love. By his death on the cross he has broken the causes of its grip on people's lives and has brought new hope.

Despite the mystery of pain and suffering—even in the middle of them—here are certainties to hold on to in a world of turmoil.

chapter

⑥

"Christianity can't be the only way to God"

Among many different kinds of obstacles that people talk about, this is one of the most common. Many people we spoke to in our survey said that they found it difficult to believe that Christianity could be unique.

- "There are too many other religions."
- "We don't really know if Christianity is true or if any religion is true."
- "I believe that God exists but that everyone has a different name for him. I think Christ existed, but I also believe that all my beliefs are true, too."—*Hindu, early twenties*

The question about truth kept coming up.

- "I believe in a "God," but to say Christianity is the true religion rather than Islam, Judaism, or Buddhism is hypocritical."

Some felt bewildered by the whole thing.

- "So many groups all claim they can lead us to God and that they're right."

Where should we start? Do all religions lead to God? Does it matter?

Different views

I love traveling.

It's the excitement of new places—the color of the stone in the buildings, the dress of the people, and the sights, sounds, and smells that make that particular place unique. Traveling always seems to leave very permanent memories. They get filed away in my mind, ready to be pulled out and lived again.

Before we had children I even enjoyed getting to these places!

It's the sensation of motion, of speed, that makes travel enjoyable. It could be a car, a train, or a plane. It doesn't much matter. The adrenalin is pumping. It lifts the spirit. It flashes new thoughts and ideas through the brain. It sparks the imagination.

Think for a moment about traveling, about getting to places. Imagine that you and I are going to travel to a particular place and meet there. Say, for the sake of argument, that it's the Eiffel Tower in Paris, and we'll meet at a particular time at the ticket booth in front of the elevator. We both live in the same place (say New York City), but for various reasons we shall be traveling separately.

The fact that we are making our separate ways to this place doesn't really matter because we both know exactly where we are going. We know roughly where Paris is, even if we haven't been there before. And we know the Eiffel Tower. It's a world-famous landmark that everyone knows about. We've seen photographs of it, so we shouldn't have too many problems once we get to Paris.

It also doesn't matter which way either of us goes. There is probably an infinite number of ways of getting there.

Train, boat, train. Car, airplane, car. And so on. The important thing is that we're both agreed about where and when we'll meet, and that the place where we're going to meet actually exists and can be located on a map.

Many people think about the different world religions in the same sort of way. "All religions are basically the same." "They all go in the same direction." "They are all talking about the same God."

And because they are all heading to the same destination, it doesn't really matter which one people choose because they all get there in the end.

In many ways this idea has a lot going for it—particularly today when there is such an emphasis on being tolerant and broad-minded. There are so many to choose from that there is no need to get uptight about one rather than another.

The trouble is, it just isn't true. It can't be true.

First of all, the only possible way it could be true is if there existed a general agreement between the different religions about who God actually *is* and what he's like.

But they don't agree.

Think back to our journey to the Eiffel Tower. Imagine that we're on our way there—both taking our different routes. Someone independently asks both of us to describe the place we're going to. We would probably start by saying "the Eiffel Tower." If we were asked to go on and describe this place in more detail we would probably go about it in different ways. We'd use different words. You might describe its shape. I might say that it's the tower that dominates the city of Paris. We might talk about its height. But the point is that sooner or later it would become clear that we were talking about the same thing.

But when it comes to talking to people of different faiths in order to compare our views about God, it soon becomes clear that we're *not* talking about the same thing at all. In fact most of the ideas cancel each other out rather quickly because they can't all be true at the same time.

Take the Buddhist view. The Buddha himself (who never claimed that he was God) said that he didn't know whether God even existed or not.

Or consider the Hindu view. I remember a conversation with a Hindu who described God as an "impersonal force" that exists throughout the universe and fills it. It cannot be seen but simply "exists." As one of the Hindu teachings describes it:

Since not by speech and not by thought,
Not by the eye can it be reached,
How else may it be understood,
But only when one says, "it is"?
—*Katha Upanishad*

But there is also a variety of different beliefs within Hinduism. Some picture a wide variety of gods, including Brahma the creator, Vishnu the preserver, and Shiva the destroyer.

The Muslim view is closer to Christianity in the sense that the Muslim creed states quite clearly that there is only one God. Each morning before sunrise the call goes out from the minarets saying, "There is no God but Allah." But when I ask Muslims more questions about what Allah is actually like, it soon becomes clear that he is very different from the Christian God.

The thing that is most often emphasized about Allah is that humans cannot really know what he is like. We are told that he acts in certain ways according to his own will—like sending both good and evil into the world for example. But he is quite beyond human knowledge. He is so distant and remote that it is impossible for people to relate to him in any personal way. The idea that he might reveal himself to humans is simply out of the question.

What a contrast this idea is to Christianity!

What would be blasphemy to a Muslim is actually the central belief of Christianity. It is that Jesus actually *does* show us what God is like—in human form. And he does it in such a way that we *may* come to know God personally.

So if we stand back from these different ideas, we have to say that they can't all be true. They can't even be different ways of describing the same thing. No disinterested onlooker would recognize these different ideas as describing the same reality.

God can't be many different gods and yet at the same time be only one. He can't be unknowable and yet at the same time fully reveal himself. The whole thing doesn't make sense, and it is pointless to talk as if it did.

The journey

Let's go back to the journey idea. We saw that many people think that religion is about making some sort of journey toward "God," something like making a human journey to get to a certain place.

Now, of course, if we're talking about getting to the Eiffel Tower we do have to make a journey. It will take effort on our part to get there. It means we have to spend time looking at maps, timetables, and guidebooks. We have to think about making connections and working out how to get from A to B. Sometimes it's hard work. Planes don't run on time. Timetables are changed. We forget to turn our watches forward. Sometimes we may get things wrong. We may take a wrong turn or catch the wrong plane. We may lose our direction altogether and have to start part of the journey all over again. Whatever happens, whether we get there without a hitch or whether we make all kinds of mistakes along the way, it is *we* who are getting there. It is *we* who are making the effort. If we didn't we wouldn't get there. It's as simple as that. It makes sense really because the Eiffel Tower is not going to move an inch toward us!

Most religions are just like this. They revolve around the idea that we have to get to "God" by our own effort. And if the effort is great enough then there's a chance (but no guarantee) that we'll be good enough to get there.

Buddhism
The Buddha said that if God existed at all he wasn't in the business of helping anyone to achieve the Buddhist goal of "enlightenment." It was up to the individual to make the effort. What stands in his way? Evil desires that result in pain and suffering. If these desires can be overcome through following the "Eightfold Path to Enlightenment" then a person may achieve "Nirvana," a state of total nothingness, self-annihilation.

Hinduism
The goal of the Hindu is also called "Nirvana," but it means something quite different from what it means to the Buddhist. For the Hindu the word means being reunited with "Brahma," the force mentioned earlier, which fills the entire universe. When a person is reunited with it, all individual identity is lost as he or she is taken up into a bigger reality, rather like a small drop of water falling into an ocean and being absorbed by it.

But again, an individual may only achieve this by his or her own effort. It is by a continual process of either moving up or down on the "cosmic life-cycle." Everything happens through a process of birth, life, death, and reincarnation. Whether it is up the cycle to a higher life form or down to a lower life form is decided by whether one has lived a good, moral life in the present world. If so, a person will move up. If not, he or she will move down. An individual's fate is determined by what the Hindu calls the "Law of Karma." It means that what you sow in this life, you will reap as reward or punishment in the next.

Christianity
Here we find something completely different. It's not a religion in which a person is accepted by God as a result of

achievement or effort. This would be quite impossible since God is perfect and accepts only those who are similarly perfect. No one can reach God by making any kind of effort or journey.

And this is exactly why Christianity is unique. It's not the individual who makes the journey. Christianity is all about God himself making the journey. It is he who does the traveling. Instead of a person trying to find God, it is God who comes to find him or her in the person of Jesus Christ.

You only have to compare Jesus Christ with the founders or prophets of other religions to see the startling difference. Whereas they are always pointing away from themselves and telling us to follow a particular path or program, Jesus is always pointing to himself and saying things like, "Anyone who has seen me has seen [God] the Father." "I am the way and the truth and the life. No one comes to the Father except through me." Or, more startling still, "He who rejects me rejects him [God] who sent me" (John 14:9; John 14:6; Luke 10:16).

I remember speaking at a student meeting. They'd given me the title "Do all religions lead to God?"

Before the meeting had begun five Muslims had introduced themselves to me and were sitting very attentively in the front row.

After the meeting they said to me, "We were interested in what you had to say. Could we talk more about it?"

I agreed happily, and we arranged a time the following afternoon when we would meet in their apartment in order to discuss the talk further.

Our discussion was friendly and open. I think I must have been there three hours. I remember many things that were said as we talked together. But one in particular stands out in my mind.

We'd been talking about the difference between Jesus and Mohammed. One of them said, "We in our religion consider Jesus to be a prophet, but you do not think of

Mohammed in the same way as we think of Jesus. Why is this?"

I asked if we could look together at part of the New Testament. It was the part in John's Gospel (chapter 14) where Jesus is talking with his close followers just before he was crucified. Philip, one of the disciples, was getting anxious to get at the truth. So he asked Jesus to show them God the Father so that they might be satisfied.

Jesus said to him, "Don't you know me, Philip, even after I have been among you such a long time? Anyone who has seen me has seen the Father" (John 14:9).

We looked up from the part we'd been reading, and I asked my friend, "If you believed that Jesus said those words, how would you answer the question you asked me?"

He said, "If I really believed that Jesus said that, I would be a Christian, not a Muslim."

This is really where we get to the heart of it. Is Jesus really who the Bible says he is? If he is, then it's the most important news ever.

C.S. Lewis describes the difference forcefully. He says that Jesus continually made "claims which, if not true are those of a megalomaniac, compared with whom Hitler was the most sane and humble of men. There is no half-way house and there is no parallel in other religions. . . . The idea of a great moral teacher saying what Christ said is out of the question. In my opinion the only person who can say that sort of thing is either God or a complete lunatic." Or, as another expert of world religions says, "Nowhere else had it ever been claimed that a historical founder of any religions was the one and only supreme deity."

Is Christianity just one out of many different ways to God then? Apparently not.

At least not if we take the words of Jesus seriously. For he claimed to be God's unique way of making himself known to the human race. To be in contact with him is to be in contact with God himself.

The claims of Jesus

The great prayer of the Brhadaranyaka Upanishad sums up the Hindu's search:

> Lead me from the unreal to reality.
> Lead me from darkness to light.
> Lead me from death to immortality.

But this searching by the Hindu is long and continuous. Jesus, on the other hand, claimed himself to be the *goal* of every person's spiritual quest. "I *am* the way and the truth and the life. No one comes to the Father except through me" (John 14:6). "I am the light of the world. Whoever follows me will never walk in darkness" (John 8:12). "I am the resurrection and the life. He who believes in me will live, even though he dies" (John 11:25).

It is precisely because Jesus is the unique revelation of God that he is able to do what no other religious leader claims to be able to do: he can put us right with God. He can deal with the barrier that separates a perfect God from his imperfect creatures.

This is not because I've done something good enough to earn God's favor. I never have done and never will. I fall short of my own standards, let alone those of God himself. No, the truth is far more realistic, and far more breathtaking. It's that God, in his immense mercy and love, took responsibility for my failures, and laid them on the shoulders of Jesus Christ when he died on the cross. Peter, one of Jesus' closest followers, says, in his first New Testament letter, that when Jesus died, "he *bore our sins* in his body on the cross" (1 Peter 2:24, italics mine). And he did it willingly. He knew exactly what he was doing when he faced his death and yet still went through with it. He hung in my place. He died for me. The Bible emphasizes from start to finish that this was the very purpose for which he

came into our world. The cross of Jesus is the place where
you and I can be put right with God.

Peace and intimacy

As a result I'm commanded to live in a way that reflects
God's character. My life will have new priorities. But as I
seek with God's help to live the Christian life I already
know that I have peace with God. Peace because my sins
are forgiven—no longer to be held against me. And all
because Jesus died for me.

There's nothing remotely like this in any other religion
in the world. Quite often you may find a similar diagnosis
of the human condition but never the cure. And never the
kind of peace that flows from it.

Christians are often accused of being intolerant and
arrogant when they talk about other religions. Maybe you
think I'm being arrogant as you read this. I don't mean to
be. It's just that once you've discovered the truth about
Christianity, it's hard to keep quiet about it. In fact it would
be a crime to do so.

An illustration may help. There are countless scientists
and doctors around the world trying to find a cure for
cancer. Many of them are working at it right now.

Suppose one of them found a cure.

Should she keep quiet about it? She doesn't want to
boast. She wants to encourage others by making them feel
that they're contributing something valuable. She would
certainly be exercising tolerance if she did keep quiet.

But there rightly would be an outcry if she did. She's
found the answer to a world problem, but she hasn't told
anyone about it. And meanwhile millions are dying of the
disease.

Now, of course, in real life she wouldn't remain silent.
How could she if she'd found the cure that could transform
people's lives?

It's a bit like that with the good news that Christians
believe. They may be no good at telling you about it. They

may seem pushy. But they only want to pass the news on: we can be forgiven; we can be right with God.

I felt a bit like that as I sat listening and talking to those Muslims.

"How can you know whether you are right with Allah?" I asked them.

"We can't. On the last day, Allah will take a pair of scales and hold them up. He will put our good deeds in one pan and our bad deeds in the other. Then we will see which way it tips."

■ In summary

I want to pass the good news on. We *can* be forgiven. And we can be sure about it.

Conclusion

This book has been written in an attempt to give some answers to the biggest obstacles that prevent people from believing in—or perhaps even thinking about—Christianity.

Many of the answers have concentrated on whether Christianity is TRUE or not. For this is its most important claim. It claims to be the truth about the world we live in. It claims to be the truth about who we are as human beings and to be the explanation of why we are as we are. It claims to be the truth about the future of the world and what will happen to it. It claims to be the truth about our eternal destiny.

If Christianity *is* true, you cannot afford to ignore it. It's too important for that.

Many people say these days, "It doesn't really matter what you believe so long as you are sincere about it." But think about it for a moment. Is this so?

Think about gravity for example. Sir Isaac Newton discovered the "Law of Gravity." Tradition has it that he did so when an apple fell out of a tree onto his head. He noticed that it fell down rather than up!

Now imagine someone comes to see me in my first-floor apartment and threatens to jump out of the window. It doesn't matter what he believes about gravity. If he jumps he will end up twenty feet below. He may never have thought about gravity. He may even sincerely believe that the "Law of Gravity" doesn't exist. But that will not affect the truth. If he jumps he'll get hurt!

So if it's right that Christianity is true, then it will remain true whether we believe it or not.

This book has been written to help you in the search for truth. I hope you will go on to examine the New Testament accounts of the life of Jesus for yourself. As you do so, ask yourself who Jesus Christ really is. Is it true that he was God in human form? Is it true that he rose from the dead? Is it true that one day we will stand before him as our judge? Is it true that he came to put us right with God in preparation for that day?

I hope more than anything that this book will help you in your search and that you will discover that this truth can be found in the person of Jesus Christ.

If you want to read more

For a basic introduction to Christianity:
George Carey, *Why I Believe in a Personal God: The Credibility of Faith in a Doubting Culture* (Wheaton, Ill.: Harold Shaw Publishers, 1991).

C.S. Lewis, *Mere Christianity* (New York: The MacMillan Co., 1964).

John R.W. Stott, *Basic Christianity* (Downers Grove, Ill.: Inter-Varsity Press, 1979).

For more evidence about Jesus and the reliability of the Bible (including the resurrection):
Josh McDowell, series editor, *Evidence for Faith* (Irving, Tex.: Word, Inc.)

J.N. Anderson, *The Evidence for the Resurrection* (Downers Grove, Ill: InterVarsity Press, 1979).

Josh McDowell, *Evidence That Demands a Verdict, Vol. 1* (San Bernardino, Cal.: Here's Life Publishers, 1979).

Josh McDowell, *Evidence That Demands a Verdict, Vol. 2* (San Bernardino, Cal.: Here's Life Publishers, 1981).

On the problem of suffering:

C.S. Lewis, *The Problem of Pain* (New York: The MacMillan Co., 1943).

David Watson, *Fear No Evil* (Wheaton, Ill.: Harold Shaw Publishers, 1985).

How to live and grow as a Christian:

David Watson, *Discipleship* (London: Hodder & Stoughton, 1981).

John White, *The Fight* (Downers Grove, Ill.: InterVarsity Press, 1977).

Ro Willoughby (editor), *Start Here: Daily Bible Readings for New Christians* (Downers Grove, Ill.: InterVarsity Press, 1988).

Notes

Chapter One/"There's no proof!"

1. F. Hoyle, *The Intelligent Universe* (Michael Joseph, 1983).
2. Quoted in Richard MacKenna, *God for Nothing* (London: Souvenir Press, 1984), p. 56.
3. *The Interpretation of the New Testament 1861-1961* (Oxford: University Press, 1964), p. 81.
4. C.S. Lewis, *They Stand Together* (London: Collins, 1979), p. 503.

Chapter Two/"Christianity is irrelevant"

1. Bishop Westcott, *The Gospel of the Resurrection* (5th edition, London: Macmillan, 1984), p. 137.
2. Dr. P. Lapide, *The Resurrection of Jesus* (London: SPCK, 1984), p. 13.
3. C.S. Lewis, *Miracles* (London: Bles, 1947), p. 173.
4. D. Watson, *Fear No Evil* (London: Hodder, 1984), p. 168.
5. Quoted in *Time* magazine, May 23, 1983.
6. Catherine Marshall, *Beyond Ourselves* (London: Hodder, 1969), p. 17.

Chapter Three/"I've never really thought about it"

1. Supertramp, from the album *Breakfast in America* (A&M Records, 1979).
2. From the album *Synchronicity* (Virgin Records, 1983).
3. Bob Geldoff, *Is That It?* (Hammondsworth: Penguin, 1986), p. 58.
4. Blaise Pascal, *Pensees* (English translation, Hammondsworth: Penguin, 1966), p. 146.

Chapter Five/"There's so much suffering in the world"

1. From the album *Some Great Reward* (Mute Records, 1984).
2. United Nations Educational Scientific and Cultural Organization.
3. Sally Magnussen, *The Flying Scotsman* (London: Quartet Books, 1981), p. 189.
4. *Religious Prisoners in the USSR* (Keston College: Greenfire Books, 1987), p. 64.